EMMANUEL JOSEPH

Beyond the Circuit: Human Stories from Tech Giants

Copyright © 2025 by Emmanuel Joseph

All rights reserved. No part of this publication may be reproduced, stored or transmitted in any form or by any means, electronic, mechanical, photocopying, recording, scanning, or otherwise without written permission from the publisher. It is illegal to copy this book, post it to a website, or distribute it by any other means without permission.

First edition

This book was professionally typeset on Reedsy. Find out more at reedsy.com

Contents

1. Chapter 1 — 1
2. Chapter 1: The Genesis of Dreams — 2
3. Chapter 2: Building Blocks of Innovation — 4
4. Chapter 3: The Human Side of Coding — 6
5. Chapter 4: Navigating Ethical Dilemmas — 8
6. Chapter 5: Women in Tech — 10
7. Chapter 6: Startups and the Entrepreneurial Spirit — 12
8. Chapter 7: Diversity and Inclusion — 14
9. Chapter 8: The Art of Leadership — 16
10. Chapter 9: The Impact of Technology on Daily Life — 18
11. Chapter 10: Bridging the Digital Divide — 20
12. Chapter 11: Future Visions and Predictions — 22
13. Chapter 12: Personal Reflections and Insights — 24

Chapter 1

Beyond the Circuit: Human Stories from Tech Giants

2

Chapter 1: The Genesis of Dreams

In the quiet corners of homes and bustling college dorms, the seeds of innovation took root. As young dreamers tinkered with primitive computers and coded late into the night, they envisioned a future shaped by technology. Their passion was fueled by the boundless possibilities they saw in the emerging digital world. Each line of code written was a step toward that future, filled with both hope and uncertainty.

The journey wasn't easy. Many faced skepticism from friends and family, who couldn't fathom the potential of these early technologies. Despite the doubts, they persevered, driven by an unshakeable belief in their vision. Their humble beginnings were marked by trial and error, with each failure serving as a lesson and a stepping stone.

Support came in various forms. Encouraging words from a mentor, a scholarship from a supportive institution, or simply the shared dream of a close-knit group of friends. These early relationships played a crucial role in nurturing their aspirations. Through collaboration and shared experiences, they began to see the broader picture of what could be achieved.

The first breakthroughs were small but significant. A software program that simplified tasks, a new way to connect people across distances, or a more efficient piece of hardware. These initial successes validated their efforts and spurred them on. They started to attract attention and gain a following, creating a ripple effect in the tech community.

CHAPTER 1: THE GENESIS OF DREAMS

Reflecting on their early journeys, these tech giants often speak of a profound sense of purpose. They weren't just creating technology; they were building a new world. Each step forward was a testament to their resilience and ingenuity. Their stories serve as a reminder of the power of dreams and the impact of unwavering determination.

As they transitioned from dreamers to doers, their visions began to take shape. What started as a passion project in a garage or a basement grew into something far more significant. They weren't just making products; they were creating legacies that would inspire future generations of innovators.

3

Chapter 2: Building Blocks of Innovation

Innovation is the lifeblood of the tech industry, a constant flow of creativity and ingenuity that drives progress. It's a process that requires not just technical skills, but also a deep understanding of human needs and desires. Tech giants have long understood this, and their stories are filled with moments of insight and inspiration.

Breakthrough ideas often come from unexpected places. A chance conversation, a late-night brainstorming session, or a sudden realization during a routine task. These eureka moments are the spark that ignites the fire of innovation. They mark the beginning of a journey that involves countless hours of development and refinement.

Collaboration is key to turning these ideas into reality. Tech giants thrive on teamwork, bringing together diverse perspectives and expertise to tackle complex challenges. The stories of successful tech projects are often stories of collaboration, where the whole is greater than the sum of its parts. Each team member brings unique skills and insights, contributing to the overall success.

Failure is an inevitable part of the innovation process. Many groundbreaking technologies were born out of failed attempts and setbacks. These experiences teach valuable lessons and build resilience. Tech giants embrace failure as a learning opportunity, understanding that each misstep brings them closer to success.

CHAPTER 2: BUILDING BLOCKS OF INNOVATION

Resilience and perseverance are essential qualities for innovators. The road to success is rarely smooth, and the ability to overcome obstacles and keep pushing forward is crucial. Tech giants often speak of the importance of staying focused on their goals, even in the face of adversity. Their stories inspire others to stay the course and keep striving for excellence.

Innovation is a never-ending journey. As technology continues to evolve, so too do the challenges and opportunities. Tech giants remain at the forefront, constantly pushing the boundaries of what's possible. Their stories remind us that innovation is not a destination but a continuous process of exploration and discovery.

4

Chapter 3: The Human Side of Coding

Behind the lines of code and complex algorithms lies a deeply human story. Programmers and software developers are the architects of the digital age, and their lives are a blend of creativity, logic, and perseverance. Their daily routines are a testament to their dedication and passion for technology.

Balancing work and life in the tech industry can be challenging. The fast-paced nature of the industry demands long hours and intense focus. Yet, many find joy and fulfillment in their work, driven by the excitement of creating something new. They find ways to manage their time and maintain a healthy balance, often relying on supportive work environments and understanding colleagues.

The culture within tech teams is unique, characterized by camaraderie and collaboration. Developers often work in close-knit groups, sharing ideas and solving problems together. This sense of community fosters innovation and creativity. Many tech professionals speak of the friendships and bonds formed through their work, highlighting the importance of teamwork.

Mental health and burnout are significant concerns in the tech industry. The pressure to perform and the constant drive for innovation can take a toll on individuals. Tech giants are increasingly recognizing the need to address these issues, promoting mental health awareness and providing resources for support. Stories of personal struggles and triumphs in this area are both inspiring and instructive.

Personal growth and career development are integral parts of the journey for many tech professionals. They continually seek to improve their skills and knowledge, driven by a passion for learning and growth. Mentorship and continuous education play crucial roles in this process, helping individuals reach their full potential.

The future of coding is bright, with endless possibilities and opportunities. As technology continues to advance, the role of programmers and developers will remain central. Their stories remind us of the human element behind the technology we use every day and the profound impact they have on shaping the world.

5

Chapter 4: Navigating Ethical Dilemmas

The tech industry is fraught with ethical challenges, from data privacy to the impact of artificial intelligence on society. Tech giants often find themselves at the center of these dilemmas, grappling with the moral implications of their innovations. Their stories offer valuable insights into the complexities of ethical decision-making.

Whistleblowers play a crucial role in highlighting ethical concerns within tech companies. Their courage to speak out against wrongdoing often comes at great personal risk. Stories of whistleblowers provide a glimpse into the darker side of the industry, revealing the challenges of holding powerful entities accountable.

The impact of technology on society and privacy is a major ethical concern. As tech companies collect and process vast amounts of data, questions about consent, security, and usage arise. Tech giants are increasingly under scrutiny for their data practices, and their responses to these concerns are shaping the future of digital ethics.

Addressing ethical concerns requires a multifaceted approach. Tech giants are implementing policies and practices to ensure ethical standards are met. This includes transparency in data usage, ethical AI development, and responsible innovation. Their efforts demonstrate a commitment to balancing innovation with moral responsibility.

The balance between innovation and ethical responsibility is a delicate one. Tech giants must navigate the fine line between pushing boundaries and respecting societal norms. Their stories highlight the importance of ethical considerations in the development and deployment of new technologies.

The dialogue about ethics in technology is ongoing. Tech giants are continuously evolving their practices to meet new challenges and expectations. Their stories serve as a reminder of the need for vigilance and integrity in the pursuit of technological advancement.

6

Chapter 5: Women in Tech

The journey of women in the tech industry is one of resilience and determination. Despite facing significant challenges, women have made remarkable contributions to technology. Their stories are a testament to the power of perseverance and the importance of diversity in the tech world.

Gender biases and stereotypes have long been barriers for women in tech. Overcoming these challenges requires not only personal strength but also systemic change. Women in tech often speak of the need for supportive environments and equal opportunities. Their experiences highlight the ongoing struggle for gender equality in the industry.

Success stories of pioneering women in tech are both inspiring and motivating. From early trailblazers to modern-day leaders, these women have made significant contributions to the field. Their achievements serve as a source of inspiration for the next generation of women in technology.

Mentorship and support networks play a vital role in the success of women in tech. Experienced professionals provide guidance and encouragement to those entering the field. These relationships foster a sense of community and help women navigate the challenges of the tech industry.

Initiatives and programs promoting diversity and inclusion are crucial for creating a more equitable tech environment. Companies and organizations are increasingly recognizing the value of diverse teams and are implementing strategies to support women in tech. These efforts are making a meaningful impact and paving the way for future generations.

Inspiring the next generation of women in technology is essential for the continued growth and innovation of the industry. By sharing their stories and experiences, women in tech are empowering others to pursue their passions and break down barriers. Their legacy is one of courage, determination, and progress.

7

Chapter 6: Startups and the Entrepreneurial Spirit

The entrepreneurial spirit is at the heart of the tech industry, driving innovation and creating new opportunities. Startups are the embodiment of this spirit, characterized by ambition, creativity, and resilience. Their stories offer valuable lessons on the highs and lows of the entrepreneurial journey.

Founding a startup is an exhilarating experience. Entrepreneurs often speak of the thrill of bringing an idea to life and the excitement of building something from the ground up. The early stages of a startup are filled with passion and energy, as founders work tirelessly to turn their vision into reality.

The journey of entrepreneurship is not without its challenges. The highs of early success can be accompanied by the lows of setbacks and failures. Startups often face significant obstacles, from securing funding to scaling their operations. The resilience and determination of entrepreneurs are key factors in overcoming these challenges.

Success stories of innovative startups that made it big are both inspiring and instructive. These stories highlight the importance of creativity, persistence, and strategic thinking. They also emphasize the role of timing

Success stories of innovative startups that made it big are both inspiring and

CHAPTER 6: STARTUPS AND THE ENTREPRENEURIAL SPIRIT

instructive. These stories highlight the importance of creativity, persistence, and strategic thinking. They also emphasize the role of timing, market understanding, and adaptability in achieving success. By analyzing these stories, aspiring entrepreneurs can learn valuable lessons and avoid common pitfalls.

The role of investors, incubators, and accelerators is crucial in the startup ecosystem. These entities provide the necessary resources, mentorship, and support to help startups grow and scale. Stories of successful collaborations between startups and investors highlight the importance of trust, shared vision, and strategic guidance. These partnerships often determine the trajectory of a startup's journey.

Lessons learned from startup failures are equally important. Not every venture will succeed, and failure is often a part of the entrepreneurial journey. These stories offer insights into the challenges and risks involved in building a startup. They emphasize the importance of resilience, learning from mistakes, and pivoting when necessary. Failure is not the end but a step towards eventual success.

The future of startups and entrepreneurship in tech is filled with promise and potential. As technology continues to evolve, new opportunities emerge for innovative ideas and ventures. The entrepreneurial spirit remains a driving force in the tech industry, fostering innovation and progress. Aspiring entrepreneurs are inspired by the stories of those who have come before them, ready to embark on their own journeys.

8

Chapter 7: Diversity and Inclusion

Diversity and inclusion are critical for the growth and innovation of the tech industry. A diverse workforce brings varied perspectives, ideas, and experiences, driving creativity and problem-solving. Tech giants are increasingly recognizing the value of diversity and are implementing strategies to promote inclusivity.

Personal stories of underrepresented groups in tech highlight the challenges they face and the progress being made. These stories emphasize the importance of creating supportive and inclusive environments where everyone can thrive. They also shed light on the systemic barriers that need to be addressed to achieve true diversity.

Efforts and initiatives to promote inclusivity are making a meaningful impact. Companies are adopting policies and practices that encourage diversity in hiring, retention, and advancement. Programs focused on mentorship, education, and community building are helping to create a more inclusive tech industry. These efforts are paving the way for a more equitable future.

The impact of diverse teams on innovation is profound. Research shows that diverse teams are more creative and effective at solving complex problems. Stories of successful projects led by diverse teams highlight the benefits of inclusivity. These stories inspire other organizations to prioritize diversity in their own teams.

CHAPTER 7: DIVERSITY AND INCLUSION

Challenges and successes in achieving diversity are part of the ongoing journey. While progress has been made, there is still work to be done. Stories of both triumphs and setbacks provide valuable insights into the complexities of creating a truly inclusive tech industry. They remind us that change is possible with commitment and effort.

The journey towards a more inclusive tech world is ongoing. Tech giants continue to evolve their practices and policies to meet the challenges of diversity and inclusion. Their stories serve as a reminder of the importance of perseverance and the positive impact that inclusive practices can have on the industry.

9

Chapter 8: The Art of Leadership

Leadership in the tech industry is a blend of vision, empathy, and strategic thinking. Effective tech leaders possess qualities that inspire and motivate their teams. Their stories provide valuable lessons on the art of leadership in a rapidly changing industry.

Inspiring leadership stories from tech giants highlight the qualities and traits of effective leaders. These leaders are known for their ability to communicate a clear vision, build strong teams, and navigate challenges with resilience. Their stories offer insights into the skills and mindsets required to lead successfully in the tech world.

The challenges of leading in a rapidly changing industry are significant. Tech leaders must stay ahead of technological advancements, market shifts, and competitive pressures. Their stories emphasize the importance of adaptability, continuous learning, and strategic decision-making. They also highlight the need for leaders to be agile and responsive to change.

Strategies for fostering a positive organizational culture are crucial for effective leadership. Tech leaders understand the importance of creating an environment where employees feel valued, supported, and motivated. Stories of successful leaders illustrate the impact of positive culture on team performance and innovation. These leaders prioritize open communication, collaboration, and professional development.

The role of empathy and emotional intelligence in leadership cannot be overstated. Tech leaders who demonstrate empathy and emotional intelligence are better equipped to understand and address the needs of their teams. Their stories highlight the importance of building strong relationships, listening actively, and providing support. Empathy-driven leadership fosters trust, loyalty, and engagement.

The evolution of leadership styles in the tech world is ongoing. As the industry continues to evolve, so too do the approaches to leadership. Stories of tech leaders adapting to new challenges and embracing innovative leadership styles provide valuable insights. These leaders are paving the way for the future of leadership in the tech industry, emphasizing the importance of adaptability and continuous improvement.

10

Chapter 9: The Impact of Technology on Daily Life

Technology has transformed nearly every aspect of daily life, from how we communicate to how we work, learn, and play. The stories of individuals whose lives have been changed by technology offer a glimpse into the profound impact of these advancements.

Everyday activities have been revolutionized by technology. From smart home devices to mobile apps, technology has made tasks more convenient and efficient. Stories of individuals using technology to enhance their daily routines highlight the benefits of these innovations. These stories also emphasize the role of technology in improving quality of life.

The positive and negative effects of technology on society are complex and multifaceted. While technology has brought numerous benefits, it has also introduced challenges such as digital addiction, privacy concerns, and the digital divide. Personal stories shed light on both the advantages and drawbacks of technological advancements, providing a balanced perspective.

The role of technology in education, healthcare, and communication is particularly significant. Tech innovations have transformed how we learn, access medical care, and connect with others. Stories of individuals and communities benefiting from these advancements illustrate the potential of technology to drive positive change. These stories inspire continued efforts to leverage technology for the greater good.

Balancing digital and real-world interactions is an ongoing challenge. As technology becomes more integrated into our lives, finding a healthy balance is essential. Stories of individuals navigating this balance offer valuable insights and strategies. They emphasize the importance of mindfulness, intentional use of technology, and maintaining meaningful real-world connections.

The future of technology's impact on daily life holds endless possibilities. As new innovations emerge, the potential for further transformation is immense. Stories of tech visionaries and futurists provide a glimpse into what lies ahead. These stories inspire curiosity, exploration, and excitement for the future of technology.

11

Chapter 10: Bridging the Digital Divide

The digital divide is a pressing issue that affects millions of people worldwide. Understanding its consequences and finding solutions to bridge the gap are critical for creating a more equitable tech world. Stories of communities and individuals striving to overcome this challenge offer valuable insights.

The digital divide refers to the gap between those who have access to technology and those who do not. This divide has significant implications for education, employment, and overall quality of life. Stories of individuals and communities affected by the digital divide highlight the urgent need for action. These stories provide a human perspective on the impact of unequal access to technology.

Efforts to bridge the digital divide are making a meaningful difference. Tech giants, governments, and non-profit organizations are implementing programs to provide access to technology and digital literacy training. Stories of successful initiatives demonstrate the power of collaboration and innovation in addressing this issue. These stories inspire continued efforts to ensure digital inclusion for all.

Innovative solutions are key to bridging the digital divide. From affordable internet access to community tech centers, creative approaches are being developed to connect underserved populations. Stories of innovative solutions showcase the potential for technology to drive positive change.

CHAPTER 10: BRIDGING THE DIGITAL DIVIDE

These stories highlight the importance of thinking outside the box and leveraging technology for social good.

The impact of connectivity on education and opportunities is profound. Access to technology opens doors to knowledge, skills, and economic opportunities. Stories of individuals who have benefited from digital inclusion emphasize the transformative power of technology. These stories inspire continued efforts to provide access to technology for all.

The vision for a more digitally inclusive world is one where everyone has the opportunity to participate in and benefit from the digital age. Stories of progress and success in bridging the digital divide offer hope and motivation. They remind us of the importance of commitment, collaboration, and innovation in creating a more equitable tech world.

12

Chapter 11: Future Visions and Predictions

The tech industry is constantly evolving, with new advancements and possibilities on the horizon. Expert predictions about the future of tech offer a glimpse into the potential of emerging technologies. Stories of visionaries and futurists provide valuable insights into what lies ahead.

The evolving landscape of technology is filled with exciting possibilities. From advancements in artificial intelligence to the potential of quantum computing, the future of tech holds immense promise. Stories of cutting-edge research and development highlight the innovative spirit driving these advancements. These stories inspire curiosity and excitement for the future.

Expert predictions about the future of tech offer valuable insights into emerging trends and possibilities. Visionaries and thought leaders provide forecasts based on current developments and future potential. These predictions help us understand the direction of the industry and prepare for what lies ahead. Stories of expert predictions offer a roadmap for navigating the future.

The role of artificial intelligence and machine learning is particularly significant. These technologies have the potential to revolutionize various industries and aspects of daily life. Stories of AI and machine learning

CHAPTER 11: FUTURE VISIONS AND PREDICTIONS

applications provide a glimpse into their transformative potential. These stories highlight the importance of ethical considerations and responsible development.

The potential of emerging technologies like blockchain and quantum computing is immense. These technologies have the power to reshape industries and solve complex problems. Stories of groundbreaking research and applications showcase the possibilities of these innovations. These stories inspire continued exploration and investment in emerging technologies.

Ethical considerations of future tech advancements are critical. As technology continues to evolve, so too do the ethical challenges. Stories of ethical dilemmas and responsible innovation emphasize the importance of balancing progress with moral responsibility. These Preparing for a tech-driven future requires foresight and adaptability. The stories of those who are at the forefront of technological advancements offer valuable lessons on navigating the complexities of an ever-changing landscape. Their insights help us anticipate future challenges and opportunities, fostering a proactive and innovative mindset.

13

Chapter 12: Personal Reflections and Insights

The personal reflections of tech leaders and innovators provide a glimpse into their unique journeys and experiences. These stories are filled with lessons learned, wisdom gained, and the impact of their work on their personal lives. They offer valuable insights into the human side of technology and the qualities that drive success.

Lessons learned from their journeys are often characterized by resilience, adaptability, and a willingness to embrace change. Tech leaders share stories of overcoming obstacles, learning from failures, and continuously striving for excellence. These lessons inspire others to persevere and pursue their passions with determination.

The impact of their work on their personal lives is a common theme in these reflections. Balancing professional achievements with personal fulfillment is a challenge faced by many tech leaders. Their stories highlight the importance of maintaining a sense of purpose, prioritizing well-being, and nurturing relationships. These reflections offer valuable insights into achieving a harmonious balance between work and life.

The legacy that tech leaders hope to leave behind is shaped by their contributions to the industry and society. Their stories emphasize the importance of giving back, mentoring the next generation, and fostering a culture of innovation and inclusivity. They aspire to create a lasting impact that inspires and empowers future innovators.

Encouraging the next generation of tech enthusiasts is a central theme in these personal reflections. Tech leaders understand the importance of nurturing talent and providing opportunities for growth. Their stories highlight the value of mentorship, education, and support in fostering the next wave of innovation. They offer words of encouragement and advice to aspiring tech professionals.

Final thoughts on the human side of technology emphasize the interconnectedness of innovation and humanity. Tech leaders reflect on the profound impact of their work on society and the responsibilities that come with it. Their stories inspire a thoughtful and ethical approach to technology, ensuring that advancements benefit all of humanity.

Beyond the Circuit: Human Stories from Tech Giants

In the high-octane world of technology, where innovation and progress seem to be the only constants, there lies a deeply human narrative often overshadowed by the sheen of digital marvels. "Beyond the Circuit: Human Stories from Tech Giants" delves into the rich tapestry of personal journeys, ethical dilemmas, and the indomitable spirit of individuals who drive the tech industry forward.

This captivating book explores the genesis of dreams that led tech visionaries from humble beginnings to the pinnacles of success. It reveals the collaborative efforts and innovative spark that birthed some of the most groundbreaking technologies of our time. Readers will gain an intimate look into the daily lives of programmers and developers, understanding the challenges they face and the culture that fosters their creativity.

Ethical questions and moral crossroads are navigated with care, highlighting the delicate balance between progress and responsibility. The book celebrates the achievements of pioneering women in tech, the struggles they overcame, and the legacy they continue to build. The entrepreneurial spirit is brought to life through stories of startups that dared to dream big and the lessons learned along the way.

"Diversity and Inclusion" sheds light on the importance of varied perspectives in driving innovation, while "The Art of Leadership" offers insights into the qualities that define successful leaders in a rapidly evolving industry. The book also explores how technology impacts daily life, bridging the digital divide, and what the future holds for tech advancements.

Through personal reflections and insights from industry leaders, "Beyond the Circuit" provides a holistic view of the human side of technology. It's a celebration of the people behind the code, the innovators who dare to dream, and the stories that inspire a tech-driven future.

www.ingramcontent.com/pod-product-compliance
Lightning Source LLC
LaVergne TN
LVHW020741090526
838202LV00057BA/6167